INSTANT BLUES

Music composed, arranged, and produced by
Douglas P. Booth with Les Horan and Layla Horan

■

Recorded at the Digital Soul Booth in New York City

■

Keyboards and rhythm—Douglas P. Booth and
Les Horan

Saxophone—Roger Byam

Guitar—Michael Hill

Harmonica—Tony Sky

INSTANT

BLUES

Les and Layla Horan

Artwork by Ulrike Kerber

St. Martin's Press
New York

Library of Congress Cataloging-in-Publication Data

Instant blues / Les and Layla Horan.
          p.   cm.—(The Play by Ear series)
        Method for piano.
        ISBN 0-312-09315-2
        1. Piano—Methods (Blues)—Instruction
and study. 2. Blues (Music)—Instruction and
study. I. Horan, Layla. II. Series.
MT239.I57   1993
786.2′1643143—dc20   93-15058
                                 CIP
                               MN

First Edition: July 1993

10 9 8 7 6 5 4 3 2 1

For Gabriel and Kaila

Contents

Introduction

The Magical Language of the Blues

Blues is the root of practically every popular musical style of the twentieth century. Its influence can be found in rock and roll, country, jazz, even today's dance music. And there is probably no music as contagious, as much fun to listen to, dance to, or play, as the blues.

The simplicity of its music and the sincerity of its lyrics combine to make the blues a deeply personal, yet universal, form of musical expression. It's a mystical kind of language all its own, a nonintellectual form of musical communication that seems to speak to its listeners on a primal, soul level.

Blues singers strike a chord in all of us when recounting the bottomless depth of their personal tragedies through song. Yet even the saddest of stories, when told within the inspirational musical format of the blues, somehow manage to make us feel good.

While much of the history of the blues never was recorded, the seeds of this musical art form can be found in the call-and-response pattern of African tribal music, in which a lead singer "called" out a musical idea and was "responded" to by a group.

The evolution of the blues as a vocal form of music continued in the rural South in the work songs, field hollers, and spirituals through which slaves lamented their suffering and sought relief and resolution.

Eventually the blues expanded from a purely vocal musical style to instrumental. Self-taught musicians originally performed on dilapidated instruments, which resulted in the honky-tonk sound still characteristic of the blues today. In time these musicians carried the blues from the raucous barrelhouses of New Orleans along the Mississippi to other parts of the country.

The special regional flavors that blues styles took on as they developed in cities such as Memphis, Kansas City, St. Louis, and Chicago combine to make the blues the uniquely American form of musical expression that is so well loved and appreciated throughout the world today.

We've put together a sampling of many different styles of blues on our background tape to give you an opportunity to explore and experience firsthand just what it means to speak the magical language of the blues!

INSTANT BLUES

Chapter 1
You're a Blues Musician

You may not know it yet, but *you can play the blues!*

You're probably thinking, Sure, I've always wanted to play the blues. But learning all those notes and chords, practicing scales and exercises for hours and hours—that stuff takes years! *I just don't have the time.*

Well, once you flip on the tape, watch your fingers glide across the keyboard, and listen with astonishment to yourself actually improvising great-sounding blues melodies, you just may find yourself having so much fun that *you won't have time for anything else!*

You're about to make the amazing discovery that it *is* possible for you to experience the truly magical world of the blues first-hand, without hours of practicing, without years of lessons, but right away, from the minute you begin! All you have to do is follow the few simple guidelines in this chapter.

1

Sound Too Good to Be True?

■ Well, just wait, because in a few minutes, so will *you!*

We know it's hard to believe, but we've seen it happen time and again. You see, we've been using the Instant Blues system with hundreds of people in workshops over the years. While we're accustomed to the skeptical glances that these promises initially bring, we've watched this skepticism melt into sheer delight just as quickly as we're able to get these doubtful folks up to the keyboard.

The Case of the Missing Melody

■ When you listen to the tape that accompanies this book, what you will hear is background music done in many different styles of blues: sometimes lively, sometimes lilting, sometimes gutsy, sometimes subdued—but unfailingly, invariably, inevitably, swinging!

What you *won't* hear, except for little smatterings here and there to help guide you, is the most important component of a tune—the melody. The *melody* is the portion of a song that brings the music to life, that holds it together, that makes it recognizable and unique. It's the part of your favorite song that you find yourself humming as you walk down the street. And this is where *you* come in. *You'll be making the melodies!*

2

That Old Black Magic

■ Here's how it works. We've arranged the pieces on Side 1 so that as you play any combination of *black keys* along with the backgrounds, your music will magically become a blues melody!

We've designed the system in this way so that you don't have to *think* about a thing. Your job is simply to relax, play around on the black keys, and create melodies that sound and feel good to you.

It's just as easy as that! All you have to do is:

1. Turn on Side 1 of the tape;
2. Listen to the music;
3. Play on the black keys.

Not for Keyboards Only!

■ By the way, if you play an instrument other than keyboard, don't let all this talk about black keys and white keys discourage you. You can play along on any instrument. Just find the instructions for your particular instrument in chapter 12, then read the book and jam along with us!

Some Hands-on Experience

■ Throughout the book we'll be recommending several easy techniques to try with the various pieces and offering lots of hints to help the melodies you improvise sound even better, even bluesier.

Later we'll be showing you how you can get some great sounds using white keys along with Side 2 of the tape, and even how to *combine* black and white keys for a still more sophisticated and authentic blues sound.

But for now, start out by experimenting just on the black keys. Play around with the pieces on Side 1. Give yourself a chance to get a sense of just how much fun playing the blues can be.

Here are a few tips to help get you started.

Tune Up

In order for the music you'll be making to sound as good as possible, your instrument should be reasonably in tune with the tape. Here's how to make sure that yours is in tune.

Below is a diagram of a keyboard. Before turning on Side 1 of the tape, find the note that is indicated on the diagram below. There are many clusters of three black keys on your keyboard. Choose one toward the center of your keyboard. Then play the white key that is located between the second and third black keys.

A

4

Those of you who know the names of the notes on the keyboard will recognize this key as A. (Throughout the book, when referring to specific notes we'll give the names of the notes for those of you who know them as well as picture diagrams for those of you who don't.)

Now turn on Side 1 of the tape. You will hear the note A repeated several times. (This note will also be repeated at the beginning of Side 2 of the tape.) Play this note on your keyboard.

If the two notes sound the same or only slightly different, you're in good shape (your ear will adjust if there's only a minor difference). If they clash, first double check to make sure you're playing the right note. If they still sound very different, *don't panic!* It's an easy situation to remedy.

1. Try a different tape deck. Yours may not be running at the appropriate speed.

2. If you're using an electronic keyboard, try adjusting the tuning knob.

3. If you're using an acoustic piano, you probably need to have it tuned.

Get Loose

Take some deep breaths, shake out your arms. Get yourself comfortable, relaxed, and ready to play.

Get in the Groove

Put on "Kansas Boogie," the first piece on Side 1. Adjust the volume so that you have a comfortable balance between the music on the tape and your own playing. Then just listen for a while. Grab the beat by tapping your foot, or snapping your fingers, or clapping your hands to the music.

Play on the Black Keys

Once you're "in the groove," put your *right hand* on the *black keys* and start to play along. At first stick mainly with the black keys toward the right of your keyboard, as that's where melodies are usually played. Later we'll take a look at chords and bass notes, which are usually played with the left hand and on the lower (left) half of the keyboard.

Have Fun with It

Put your intellect on hold! There'll be plenty of time for explanations and instructions later on. For now don't try too hard or think too much—just *play*.

Do It Your Way!

■ While this book is filled with suggestions, keep in mind that there really is no "right" way to approach this.

Some beginners like to start slow and easy, letting their creativity blossom gently and delicately as they gain confidence at the keyboard. If this is you, you may choose to keep your melodies very simple and sparse, playing just a few notes and using only one finger.

Others like to start right out by attacking the keys with fervor, pushing themselves to the outermost limits of their creativity, into full-tilt musical "enlightenment."

So pick your "poison." Just don't forget to *listen to the music as you play*. A good way to keep in touch with the music is to think of your fingers as little dancers on a "stage" of piano keys.

Play along with any or all of the pieces on Side 1 as many times as you wish. And don't feel restricted by the order that we've chosen for the backgrounds. For instance, if the first piece, which is rather upbeat, feels too difficult or simply doesn't suit your particular taste or mood at the moment, skip it for now and come back to it later. Side 1 is packed with a wide variety of blues styles and tempos, and *all* of them sound good with black keys.

Remember, the suggestions we've given you here are merely intended to give you a jump start.

But all you really need to get started is a hand (even a finger will do), a keyboard, and a desire to play the blues!

Chapter 2
The Joy of Jamming

If you followed the simple instructions in chapter 1 and played along with the tape, selecting notes as you went along, what you were doing was improvising, or as musicians call it, *jamming*.

Musical Doodling

■ *Improvisation* is simply an exploration of the notes on your instrument. It's generally done without any particular result in mind, kind of like doodling on a pad of paper.

Aside from being fun, improvisation can be a highly creative and profoundly valuable means of expression. In fact, it's from this form of musical experimentation that virtually all songs are born.

It's likely that whoever wrote your favorite song began by sitting at an instrument and searching through combinations of notes. When their experimentation uncovered the beginnings of a melody that "caught their ear," they continued to build on it, searching for more and more notes until finally all of the notes they put together developed into a cohesive tune.

Play Like a Pro!

■ When professional musicians jam together they have a good idea of what the notes they're about to play will sound like, as they have a solid understanding of chords, scales, and music theory, not to mention years of experience on their instruments. And since professionals are free to mix and match all of the notes on the keyboard, they have a wide variety of choices.

With *Instant Blues* we've dramatically simplified your choices by limiting you to only the particular combinations of notes that sound best with the specific pieces you'll be playing along with. In some cases that will be only black keys, in others only white, and in still others a simple combination of both.

While you may not yet have the freedom of a professional blues musician to pick and choose from notes above and beyond the ones we'll be giving you, if you follow the system you'll be choosing from the same bank of notes that would *predominate* in his or her playing. That's how it's possible for the notes you play to sound so surprisingly professional.

You Don't Have to Pay Your Dues If You Want to Play the Blues

■ Becoming a master blues musician, or for that matter any kind of musical superstar, demands such intense work and dedication that only a few sturdy, persistent souls have the patience to tough it out. Most people simply give up long before having a chance to experience the joy of making music.

While we certainly can't promise that *Instant Blues* will transform you into a musical giant replete with limos and private jets, we *can* promise you a gratifying, fulfilling musical experience—and an awful lot of fun to boot!

The "magical" system we've developed makes the joy of playing the blues accessible to *everyone*, not only to the superstars of the world.

Take It from the Top

■ Approaching music in the way that we offer it to you in this book is sort of like starting at the top. You'll have a rare opportunity to enjoy the musical rewards that years of hard work would bring—*before* you've put in any hard work at all.

This is very different from the way learning music is usually approached. Normally you start out at the very "bottom" of the process, struggling through labor-intensive years of scales, drills, and music theory. Only after mastering all of the little steps along the way do you finally find yourself at the top, making music flow gracefully and effortlessly and having all the fun you were looking forward to when you first began.

Learnin' While You're Burnin'

■ That's not to say you won't learn anything from the *Instant Blues* experience. In fact, quite the opposite is true. You see, there's an extra, hidden bonus built right into the system: *without trying, without even realizing it, you'll actually be learning quite a lot about music while you're having a ball pounding out those blues riffs.*

You'll be developing rhythm, coordination, and confidence. Your ear for music will improve, as will your feel for the many different styles of the blues.

Playing in the Musical Sandbox

■ You'll be learning about music in much the same way that young children absorb information about the world around them while at play. As they romp in the sandbox, filling their pails, digging with their shovels, and building castles, they're developing coordination, gaining a sense of proportion and balance, and learning how to interact with playmates.

Similarly, as you frolic at the keyboard with *your* playmate, the *Instant Blues* cassette, you'll be gaining invaluable insight into what making music is really all about—an insight that just may change anything you ever wish to do with music in the future, whether it's playing, dancing, or listening to it.

Swing Now, Sweat Later

■ Of course, once you've explored the many varied styles of blues we've provided for you on the special tape we've included, you may find yourself so turned on to making music that you're willing, even eager, to go on and do the work it would take to become another Ray Charles, Eric Clapton, or Jerry Lee Lewis.

But the beauty of it is that you don't have to! You can begin making great-sounding blues music *immediately*, using only the tape and the hints contained in this small book.

Chapter 3
Tuning Up Your Attitude

By now you're probably starting to get the idea of what a mesmerizing experience playing the blues can be. And if you liked what you've heard so far, hold on to your piano keys! *You've only just begun!*

Of course most people, no matter *how* good they sound, want to sound even better. That's why the rest of this book is packed with some simple techniques to try along with the backgrounds and some tricks of the trade designed to help you really get your hands on that authentic, bluesy sound.

And for those of you who are haunted by the notion that your playing should sound better than it does, read on. This chapter is dedicated to casting out those nasty little demons that hide in the recesses of your mind, delivering discouraging diatribes designed to prevent you from unleashing the full power of your creativity.

In our Instant Blues workshops we've seen even "slow starters" blossom miraculously in the course of only a few hours after trying out a few of our "attitude adjustment" techniques.

Cop an Attitude!

■ Whether you're a professional who's been playing for years or a complete beginner who's never touched an instrument before, the attitude with which you approach making music is probably the single most critical factor in determining how good you'll sound.

So tune in to these few simple tips designed to tune up your attitude, and watch your playing improve by leaps and bounds.

Get Excited About It!

■ Approach this experience as a musical adventure. Embark upon it with all the excitement and enthusiasm you can muster!

Even the most brilliantly crafted melody will fall flat when delivered in a dull, timid musical monotone. But if you rev yourself up, turn yourself on, and hit those black keys as if you're playing the hottest blues piece this side of the Mississippi, you'll infuse even the simplest combinations of notes with *electricity*.

Don't Analyze or Criticize

■ There is probably nothing more destructive to creativity than criticism. So encourage your every effort, appreciate your every note!

If you're brand new to the keyboard or to the blues, you really are like a baby learning to talk or walk. Treat your first notes with the same amazement and appreciation as you would a baby's first words or steps. In the same way, your first notes really are the beginning of a remarkable journey!

Jump into a Superstar's Shoes

■ Imagination is a direct channel for creativity. We originally developed this game of make-believe for our Instant Blues workshops to loosen up some of our more reticent participants.

At first we were pleased that it seemed to accomplish our aim of coaxing these shy souls up to the keyboard to play. But after trying it out on several people we were amazed to find that this little exercise had the remarkable fringe benefit of bringing out a hidden, musical persona that astonished not only them but everyone else in the room as well. Give it a try!

As a part of getting ready to play along with the tape, pretend you really *are* Billy Joel, or Aretha Franklin, or Stevie Wonder, or any of your idols, backstage, about to perform for a crowd of thousands. Muster every ounce of your charm, charisma, and confidence. Then get out there on that stage, sit down at your instrument, and knock 'em dead!

We aren't exactly sure *why* this technique works so well in summoning forth people's innate musicality. We can only surmise that being someone else for a while—someone we admire and respect—is a powerful way to cast aside those stern internal judges.

This little exercise seems to give people permission to come out of their creative closet and feel free to express themselves without embarrassment or anxiety.

It Don't Mean a Thing
If It Ain't Got That Swing

■ Remember that what we're attempting to do here is add some excitement and "swing" to your playing. If you try to play fast and flashy before you're technically able you're likely to lose the beat—along with the point of the process.

The purpose of this little fantasy is to give you an opportunity to try on your idol's *attitude* for size, not mimic his or her *technique*. We aren't suggesting that you try to play as many notes as your idol might. In fact, it's *impossible* to swing if you're struggling to reach for handfuls of notes that are way beyond your grasp.

If your mind absolutely boggles at the sheer magnitude of notes that Oscar Peterson can play, remember that he's able to make all those notes sound flowing and beautiful because he's playing exactly at his own level. It's easy and effortless for him. He's not struggling, suffering, or sweating. He's just having a great time doing what comes naturally.

If you just do what comes naturally for *you* and play only as

16

many notes as are comfortable for you to handle, the same joy of making music is yours for the taking.

And keep in mind that while your playing may not sound as fast or flashy as Oscar Peterson's, even a few simple, elegantly placed notes can *really swing*. Infuse your music with soulfulness and feeling and you'll transform it into something that is both fun to play *and* fun to listen to.

Enjoy the Scenery

■ Some psychologists believe that the two halves of the brain perform very different functions and perceive reality in starkly contrasting ways.

Simply put, the left brain is the goal-oriented, "grown up" part of your consciousness that wants answers, explanations, and *results*. The right brain is the primitive, preverbal, imaginative part that just wants to lay back, hang out, and have some fun.

We'll try to provide your left brain with enough information to keep it happy and out of the way, by giving you plenty of hints that will enable you to see progress, improvement, and results.

But the real aim of *Instant Blues* is to summon the subtle and mysterious power of the right brain, which can guide you to new creative heights if you'll let it!

All you have to do is make the little leap of faith it takes to assure yourself that you will, indeed, get there—that in fact, you already *are* there as long as you let yourself relax and enjoy the wondrous process of making music.

In other words, enjoy the scenery and don't worry about the destination.

Oops!

■ "Oops" tends to be the mantra of the amateur musician. It's repeated with a nearly religious fervor just about every time the fingers refuse to do exactly as the brain instructs them.

Conversely, one of the marks of a true professional is that he or she knows how to make mistakes. It's not that pros don't make mistakes. They make lots of them. In fact, if you were a trained music critic listening to most any pro on just about any given night, you'd likely hear dozens of notes that were never intended to be played, along with a multitude of other "unexpected variations"—otherwise known as mistakes.

But the truth is that the average person will never recognize any of these mistakes. And those who *do* catch them will very likely be unperturbed by them. That's because when a professional makes a mistake, he or she knows how to get out of it gracefully.

In fact, the secret to making a "good mistake" is just that—get out of it gracefully.

If your finger slips onto a black key when it meant to light on a white one, or onto a white key when it was aiming for a black, or even if you happen to find your fingers tangled in a cluster of sour-sounding notes, stay cool!

Don't call attention to it by cursing, wringing your hands, or bringing your playing to a dead halt. Just move on.

Keep on playing and pretend it never happened!

Give Yourself Permission to Have an "Off Night"

■ In order to fuel your budding creative fires and keep your enthusiasm and excitement alive, making music must never feel like a chore.

The only "should" to keep in mind while playing along with *Instant Blues* is that it should always feel like fun. If it begins to feel like work, or if you catch yourself feeling frustrated, irritated, or bored, *get up and leave the keyboard!*

Off nights happen to the best of 'em. There's not a musician alive, no matter how famous, no matter how professional, who hasn't experienced a disappointing session at his or her instrument. So if you have an experience at the keyboard that's less than breathtaking, don't let it discourage you. Come back again later, the next day, or whenever the mood strikes you.

You may be surprised to find that a short break was all that was needed to not only restore your creative momentum but enhance it!

Chapter 4
Finger Aerobics

I n the same way that aerobics can warm up your body, strengthen your muscles, and help you develop grace, rhythm, and coordination, "finger aerobics" can help tone up your rhythmic sense and get your sluggish fingers revved up and ready to move around the keyboard.

Playing in Rhythm

■ Rhythm is the very essence of music. It's the element that makes you want to clap to it, move to it, dance to it. Most musicians agree that rhythm is the single most important element in making your music sound, well, *musical!*

In fact, a simple melody made up of only a few notes and played with the beat will sound far better than the most complex, sophisticated melody played out of rhythm.

You've Got Rhythm

■ You were first exposed to rhythm while still in the womb, through the constant, steady pulse of your mother's heartbeat. You were rocked rhythmically in your infancy, and since then that innate sense of flowing with the beat has become an integral part of your everyday existence.

You *talk* in rhythm, *walk* in rhythm, even *breathe* in rhythm! But ironically, the beginning music student often finds rhythm the most elusive aspect of music to master.

That's because when first starting out there are so many things to focus on all at the same time—deciphering the notes on a sheet of music, figuring out how to find them on your instrument, coordinating your hands—that the beginner's natural rhythmic sense can easily become distorted.

Because serious musicians understand just how vital rhythm is to making their music swing, they work hard at perfecting each and every step along the way, until playing "in time" becomes just as natural as breathing.

With *Instant Blues* we've made it possible for you to sidestep all of the struggles and distractions, at least for now. Accept this opportunity as an open invitation to your innate rhythmic sense to come through and let itself be heard!

Feeling the Beat

■ How do you know if you're playing in rhythm? Usually your instinct will tell you. In general, if you feel comfortable with what you're playing, if the melodies you're making seem to glide smoothly along with the background music, you're probably playing in rhythm.

If your playing feels awkward or "out of sync," take that as a signal to stop and listen for a while. Take a minute to get into the groove. Then when you're ready, begin playing again—*slowly* at first. Keep your playing simple and laid back until you're feeling more comfortable with the beat.

If you're brand new to making music and a little insecure about relying on your instinct just yet, you may want to use some of the following suggestions to help you "get with the beat."

Tap It, Snap It, Clap It!

■ Think of the beat as the heartbeat of a song—the rhythmic, hypnotic pulse of the music.

Put on "Kansas Boogie," the first piece on Side 1. It has a strong, obvious beat, and before the music even begins, you'll hear some solid finger snapping to help get you into the rhythm.

Listen carefully. Try to catch the beat, then go with it. Begin by tapping your foot, snapping your fingers, or clapping your hands to it. You can even try drumming your fingertips to the music on your lap or on a tabletop.

This kind of "hand jamming" can be a powerful form of musical expression in and of itself. If you've ever watched Ray Charles, Al

Jarreau, or any other musical giant energize their audience by snapping, tapping, and clapping to the music during a performance, you know what an infectious experience it can be!

So don't clap along in a halfhearted, humdrum way! Feel your whole body resonate to the pulse of the music. In other words, *get excited about it*.

Play It!

■ Now try playing some rhythms on the keyboard. Rather than tapping, snapping, or clapping to the music, *play a black note instead*. You may wish to begin by staying on only *one* black key for a while, until you feel secure with the beat.

Ease your way into it if you need to. Add notes and fingers as you feel able. And you needn't limit yourself to the right hand only. Some beginners like to drum rhythmically with the fingers of both hands. Anything goes! Just try to stay in touch with the rhythm as you play.

Leave Space!

■ One good way for a beginner to get a handle on the rhythm of a piece is to play a note on *every* beat. Of course, if you were to do that continually, with no change in the rhythmic pattern at all, it would become a little monotonous after a while.

Rhythmic variations are what make music interesting! Experiment with the rhythm by playing a note on some beats and resting, or leaving space, on others.

Here are some examples of rhythmic combinations you can use. A dash indicates a rest on that particular beat.

BEAT	BEAT	BEAT	BEAT
Play	—	Play	—

BEAT	BEAT	BEAT	BEAT
—	Play	—	Play

BEAT	BEAT	BEAT	BEAT
Play	Play	—	Play

BEAT	BEAT	BEAT	BEAT
—	Play	Play	—

Variations on the Theme

■ Make up your own rhythmic combinations. The possibilities are endless, which is what makes improvising so much fun!

And you needn't limit yourself to just one black key for long. As you feel more confident you can begin improvising using as many notes as you can handle, playing one, two, or even three notes on every beat.

Five-Finger Jam

■ Now let's bring all five fingers into play. For now, try the five-finger jam with your right hand, the one most often used to play melodies. Later, when we focus on playing with both hands, you may wish to come back and try some of these ideas with the *left*.

Put the fingers of your right hand in a row, on any group of five adjacent black keys, as illustrated below.

Thumb

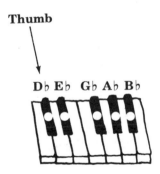

Db Eb Gb Ab Bb

If you're a beginner you may want to try this first without the background music. Starting with the thumb, play one black key at a time until you've reached the pinky. Then come back down, playing pinky, ring finger, middle finger, pointer, then thumb. Continue repeating this pattern, starting out slow and relaxed and gradually picking up speed.

Turn On the Tape

■ Now put on "Kansas Boogie" and try the five-finger jam to the music.

Experiment with rhythm. First, move up and down the keys, playing one black key on every beat, or even on every second or third beat. Then begin to vary the rhythm. Play two or more notes on some beats and rest on others. As you begin to loosen up, let yourself go and create rhythms of your own.

Improvise. After you've played straight up and down for a while, begin to improvise. Play the notes *in any order* that you wish. Tap along on the keys as if you were drumming to the music. Listen for the rhythm, always keeping in touch with the beat as you play.

Create melodies. Every combination of notes that you play is a melody. Of course, some will sound better to you than others. Even though you're somewhat limited in a five-finger position, you'll probably still be able to find melodies that are pleasing to you and sound good with the background music.

Move to the Music

■ Next try moving to other five-finger positions by shifting your hand from one set of five black keys to another. Play around for a while in one five-finger position, then move to another. Explore how your rhythmic improvisations sound in other locations on the keyboard.

If you're a complete beginner, shifting positions may feel awkward at first, so start out slowly. What you're aiming for is a smooth and graceful movement with a "direct hit" on all five keys.

Three-Finger Jam

■ If you find working with all five fingers cumbersome, you can improvise using only the first three. In fact, many blues musicians do just that, since the thumb, index finger, and middle finger are far more agile than the ring finger or pinky.

A Rule of Thumb for Moving Around the Keyboard

■ Keyboard players usually use their thumbs to help them move smoothly up and down the keyboard.

Moving Up the Keyboard

To move the right hand *up* the keyboard (to the right), cross your thumb under your middle finger.

You may want to try it first without the music. Begin on any black key and play thumb first, then index, then middle. Then bring your thumb under the middle finger and start over. Continue moving up the keyboard in this fashion.

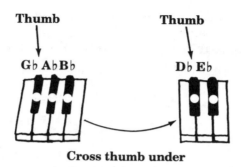

Cross thumb under

Moving Down the Keyboard

To move the right hand *down* the keyboard (to the left), simply reverse the process. Cross your middle finger over the thumb as you come down.

Begin on any black key and play the middle finger first, then index, then thumb. Then cross your middle finger over the thumb and start again, moving all the way down the keyboard.

Go with the Flow

■ Now *just jam*. Move around the keyboard sometimes using your thumb, sometimes shifting five-finger positions, and sometimes using three fingers. But mostly just playing any old way you please!

In this chapter and throughout the book we offer you these and other techniques simply as "goodies" to store in your musical bag of tricks and pull out whenever you have a taste for them. They're here to provide you with variety and some additional guidance, and help widen your musical perspective.

But don't turn them into obstacles to your creativity and spontaneity by getting hung up on them. Once you've played around with some of our suggestions, *just forget about 'em.* Go back to jamming, letting your instinct and the background music be your guides.

If you'll just *listen to the music* and stay with the beat, you'll likely hear yourself improvising some bluesy, melodic riffs!

Chapter 5
Black Magic (Side 1)

Here we'll be taking a closer look at the individual pieces on Side 1 and pointing out some things you might want to listen for as you play along.

First, here are some general ideas that can be applied to *any* of the black-key backgrounds. Of course, before trying out anything new be sure you're comfortable with the basics—playing along on the black keys with Side 1 of the tape.

On a Lighter Note

■ There is one *white* key that will feel right at home when played along with the black keys. That key is A. Locate any group of three black keys. The A is the white key between the second and third of the three black keys.

The A can lend a sweet, bluesy dissonance to your improvisations. It sounds especially nice when followed by either of the black keys directly to the right or left of it. If you need to, apply

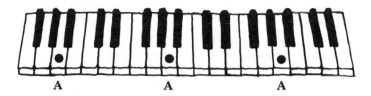

stickers or pieces of masking tape to the A's on your keyboard so that you can readily locate them.

Four-Finger Jams

■ Here are a couple of four-finger jams that sound nice along with the backgrounds on Side 1 and will help you get accustomed to using the A.

Place the thumb of the right hand on the second of any two black keys (E♭). Then place the index finger on the next black key (G♭), the middle on the next (A♭), and the ring finger on the white key (A).

Thumb

E♭   G♭ A♭

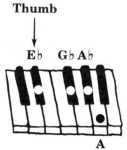

A

31

Put on any piece from Side 1 and play along on these four notes, just as you did with the "five-finger jam" in the finger aerobics chapter. Play up and down for a while, then vary the rhythm, leave space, and finally just let loose and play the notes in any order, looking for melodies that are pleasing to you.

Here's another four-finger jam. This time begin with the thumb on the white key, A, and the index, middle, and ring fingers on the next three black keys (B♭, D♭, and E♭), as illustrated below.

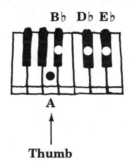

Playing Two Notes at a Time

■ Certain two-note combinations can add a fuller, even more bluesy sound to your playing. And even though this is a technique commonly used by professional blues musicians, it's surprisingly easy to do.

One combination that sounds especially nice uses the E♭ on top and any other black key, or the white key A, underneath it. Try playing these notes together along with any of the pieces on Side 1. Use any two fingers of the right hand that are comfortable for you, or play the E♭ in the right hand and the bottom note in the left.

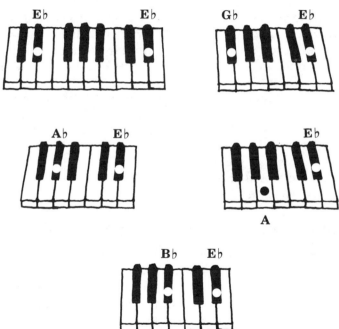

You needn't limit yourself to the E♭ on top. As you experiment with various two-note combinations you're bound to find others that you'll like.

Living Dangerously

■ While you can always count on the black keys along with the A to give you a traditional, bluesy sound, there are some other white keys you can add that will work from time to time. So if you find yourself in a devil-may-care, I-gotta-be-free kind of mood, *do it!* Experiment!

Through experimentation you're bound to come up with some new and exciting possibilities. Just don't allow yourself to become discouraged by the few "off" choices you're bound to fall into when you stray from the "safe" notes we've given you. If you find yourself not liking what you hear, you can always duck back into the "safety zone" and play the foolproof notes again for a while, then venture back out again later.

"Kansas Boogie" (Side 1, Piece 1)

"Kansas Boogie" is based on boogie-woogie, a style of playing that became popular in the United States around the 1930s. It's generally believed that boogie-woogie was originally developed in logging camps in the South. Since the pianos available were old and broken down, and since the mood of the audience was usually rowdy, musicians had to quite literally pound that piano just to be heard over the commotion. The loud, driving beat and heavy repeated bass lines are elements which still remain characteristic of boogie-woogie today.

The tempo of "Kansas Boogie" is fairly quick, but don't be put off by it! Rather than overcompensating by pushing yourself, try doing the opposite. Keep your playing sparse until you're feeling comfortable with the rhythm. If you still feel you're having trouble keeping up, come back to it once you've warmed up with some of the slower pieces.

Listen to the piano parts in the background for guidance and inspiration to carry into your own improvisations.

"Lazy Bones" (Side 1, Piece 2)

"Lazy Bones," a slow, relaxed, eight-bar blues piece, was inspired by old recordings of big brass bands, with a little gospel flavor thrown in for good measure.

A unique characteristic of this style is that the bass notes are played by a tuba rather than an acoustic guitar or bass. "Lazy Bones" has a fairly strong melody of its own that repeats every few choruses. You can either play around it or use it as an opportunity to "leave space" and simply listen to it.

"Nice 'n Easy" (Side 1, Piece 3)

"Nice 'n Easy" has a bass line reminiscent of the early days of rock and roll. However, we've sprinkled the piece with some very contemporary guitar riffs, which you can use to help get you in the groove. Use the space around the guitar riffs and vocals to explore and expand on your own improvisations. As the title implies, go nice 'n' easy. It's meant to be a slow piece, so don't rush it. In the background you may be able to hear that the chords are played in groups of three. A beat divided into three parts in this way is called a *triplet*.

"Kinda Straight" (Side 1, Piece 4)

"Kinda Straight" is in straight time, which means that each beat is divided into two or four even parts. This differs from shuffle time, which has more of a triplet feel.

Now, bypassing all of the musical jargon, you can easily *feel* the difference between straight time and shuffle time. Simply listen to the other straight time pieces on the tape, "A Minor Affair" on Side 1 and "Beat So Strong," "Let It Ride," and "Lady Honeydew" on Side 2. Then contrast the feel of the straight time beat with some of the shuffle pieces—"Kansas Boogie" on Side 1 and "Work It Out" and "Switchin' " on Side 2. You'll find yourself moving very differently to the different grooves.

"A Minor Affair" (Side 1, Piece 5)

"A Minor Affair" is a twelve-bar blues piece done in a minor key. The feel is reminiscent of B. B. King's classic *The Thrill Is*

Gone, except that instead of guitar, we feature saxophone. You'll be "trading solos," in a sense, with the sax, which drifts in and out of the piece. You'll also hear a synthesized string section holding long, sustained sounds in the background.

"Ebony Blue" (Side 1, Piece 6)

"Ebony Blue" gives you a taste of how forties and fifties jazz musicians used more complex chord changes, rhythms, and improvised melodies to transform the blues into a style all their own.

The melody of "Ebony Blue" is reminiscent in style of one of the all-time great jazz pianists, Thelonious Monk. This piece uses the format of traditional jazz tunes, in which a melody (or "head") begins the piece, followed by musicians taking turns improvising, with the head returning at the end of the piece. In "Ebony Blue," we also repeat the melody in the middle.

When the melody comes around you can "leave space" and simply listen to it, play around it, or even try to copy it. It uses these four notes. See if you can use your ear to find the order in which the notes are played. Hint: the first note is B♭.

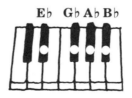

E♭ G♭ A♭ B♭

"Just One Thing" (Side 1, Piece 7)

"Just One Thing" uses just one chord throughout the entire piece. We kept it that way in order to give you a taste of two-handed playing. (More on that later in chapter 11.) For now do just one thing—jam along with the piece.

Listen for the many different instruments coming in and out, and for the texture and volume changes that we added in order to offset the monotony that can result from limiting an entire piece to only a single chord.

Chapter 6
White Magic (Side 2)

A s you'll soon discover if you haven't by now, playing on the white keys is a lot easier than playing on the black keys, since the skips are not as wide and the keys are bigger and more evenly spaced. That's the good news.

The flip side is that while all of the white notes will blend with the backgrounds, two of them—the B and E—don't always sound as authentically bluesy as the others. But with a little masking tape we'll show you how you can work around all that in just a minute.

For starters play along with some of the pieces on Side 2, using *all* of the white keys. (Save the last tune, "Switchin' " for later, as it alternates between black and white keys.)

You probably noticed that these two notes don't sound "bad" or "wrong"—just not quite as bluesy. In fact, you can get by perfectly well playing on all of the white keys. But if you want to go for a 100 percent genuine, guaranteed authentic blues sound all the way through—no B no E, no fuss no muss—this is where the masking tape comes in handy.

Simply apply pieces of tape, or more creative decals if you prefer, to the two less predictable notes, B (the white keys to the right of the groups of three black keys) and E (the white keys to the right of the groups of two black keys). This way you won't have to interrupt your creative flow by having to remember which notes to avoid.

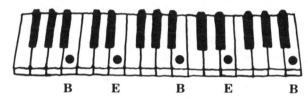

B   E   B   E   B

On a Darker Note

■ Once you're warmed up and comfortable on the white keys—and you may want to try some of the finger aerobics from chapter 4 on the white keys to help you get comfortable—you can begin adding some of these little "extras" to your improvisations.

Just as there was one white key that sounded perfectly bluesy along with the black keys for Side 1, the same can be said in reverse for Side 2. This key is A♭. Locate any group of three black keys. The A♭ is the black key right smack in the middle, and it sounds just great along with the white keys, especially when followed by either of the white keys directly to the right or left of it.

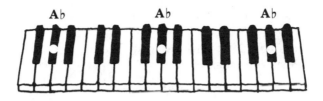

Four-Finger Jams

■ If you liked working with the black-key four-finger jams, here are a couple of four-finger jams that work well on the white keys along with the backgrounds on Side 2. Play around with these white-key four-finger positions just as you did with the black-key four-finger positions.

Place the thumb of the right hand on the white key located between any group of two black keys (D). Then, skipping a white

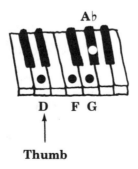

Thumb

key (E), place the index finger on the next white key (F), the middle on the next (G), and the ring finger on the black key (A♭).

Here's another. This time begin with the thumb on the black key (A♭). Place the index finger on the white key directly next to

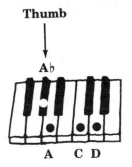

it (A). Then, skipping a white key (B), place the middle on the next white key (C) and the ring finger on the next key (D).

Playing Two Notes at a Time

■ You can get the same bluesy results as you did with the black keys by playing certain combinations of two white keys. The best note to put on top is the white note between the groups of two black keys, D. Use any two fingers of the right hand, or play the D in the right hand and the bottom note in the left.

The top note can be played with any other white key, or the black key, A♭. Then look for other combinations of white notes, eventually even experimenting with combinations that include the B and E.

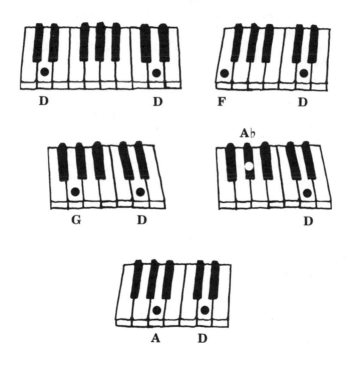

Living Dangerously

■ Again, although we've provided you with "foolproof" notes, nothing's really sacred, so experiment, explore, expand, if you want to. You can always come back to the "safety zone." In addition to the A♭ you can try adding other black notes to the white key pieces. Some will work better than others, of course. But since you know which bank of notes to bank on, you really have nothing to lose by trying!

"Beat So Strong" (Side 2, Piece 1)

"Beat So Strong" begins with a slow ad lib intro, setting the mood for the New Orleans blues feel that follows. Listen for the characteristic riffs that the horns play in the background. You may recognize the keyboard influence of some of the masters of this particular blues style, such as Professor Longhair, Dr. John, and Allen Toussaint.

"Let It Ride" (Side 2, Piece 2)

"Let It Ride" has an R and B groove. It's the only piece on the cassette done in twenty-four-bar blues, so you may get the sense that the piece is somehow more extended than the others as you play along. We'll get into why that is later, when we take a closer look at the structure of the blues. "Let It Ride" is modeled after one of the most famous twenty-four-bar blues tunes, "Mustang Sally."

This is the only piece on the cassette featuring a complete set of lyrics. You can either take center stage, using the singing as just another background instrument, or you can "step aside," making your own playing the accompaniment to the singing.

You may want to leave some space for the very special guitar playing in the middle of the piece. It's well worth giving a listen and trying to capture some of that fantastic feel in your own playing.

"Lonely Street" (Side 2, Piece 3)

"Lonely Street" has the slow, fifties triplet feel you may recognize from "Nice 'n Easy" on Side 1. Here we combined that groove with a slightly jazzier bass line and chord progression.

In the beginning of the piece and several times throughout it, you'll hear a break in the rhythm. This is called "stop time." Elvis Presley's "Heartbreak Hotel" starts off in a similar way. When you hear the band drop away and you find yourself suddenly solo, don't be thrown by it. Treat it as another exciting challenge to your creativity.

As you play you'll hear fragments of piano riffs tinkling softly in and out of the background. Use these to inspire your own melodies.

"Work It Out" (Side 2, Piece 4)

"Work It Out" is a feelin' good jitterbug groove. You'll hear shades of fifties' rockabilly and shadows of the swing music of the thirties and forties made famous by Glenn Miller, Count Basie, and Benny Goodman.

"Work It Out" also lets you trade solos or just play along with some spectacular sax riffs.

"Lady Honeydew" (Side 2, Piece 5)

"Lady Honeydew" is modeled after Herbie Hancock's "Watermelon Man." It's got a bit of a jazzy, Latin flair. Like "Ebony Blue" on Side 1, this piece begins with a melody that repeats at the end. Toward the middle you'll hear an interesting combination of two different bass parts, one playing the bass line as the other improvises melodies in the higher range.

"Tunnel Vision" (Side 2, Piece 6)

"Tunnel Vision" fades in as if from far away, gradually becoming louder as it passes through, then fading away into the distance—kind of like a train tooling through a tunnel. The harmonica accompanied only by drums, bass, and rhythm guitar gives the piece its slow, simple, easy mood, reminiscent of a Bo Diddley kind of piece.

Most people find it easy and comfortable to play with "Tunnel Vision." So easy, in fact, that in chapter 11 we'll show you how to play along with it using both hands.

"Switchin' " (Side 2, Piece 7)

"Switchin' " is a medium shuffle that we've arranged so that you can alternate between white keys and black keys. When the music starts, begin playing on the white keys. When you hear "switchin'," move to the black keys. Then, when you hear "switchin' " again, switch back to white keys, and so on. When you're on the white keys you can add the black note A♭ and when you're on the black keys you can add the white note A.

There are two ways to tell whether you're in the right place. One is simply by whether or not your playing sounds right with the background. If you're in the wrong place, it'll clash. Another clue is that the orchestrations for the white key parts differ from those for the black keys. With the exception of the last chorus, in which all of the instruments join in for a big finish, you'll hear mostly piano and an occasional harmonica in the sections that correspond to white keys. In the black key section you'll hear mostly organ and horns.

Chapter 7
Musically Speaking

W hen you listen to a brilliant political speaker, a talented trial attorney, or an inspiring religious leader, you'll hear a monologue sizzling with *style*, a symphony of sound filled with booming baritones, soft, breathy whispers, and short, spurting staccatos punctuated with long, pregnant pauses.

Often, listeners are moved by an inspired, animated delivery more than by the intellectual content of the message itself. In other words, it's not always *what* they say, but *how* they say it that makes listening to these orators such an ear-catching experience.

Musical Monologues

■ In the same way that a moving monologue is more than just a random jumble of words, expressive, "eloquent" music is more than just a random sequence of notes.

Good melody lines are cohesive. The notes hang together in a way that makes musical "sense."

Learning how to put together coherent musical thoughts is a lot like learning a foreign language. You usually begin by becoming familiar with the words one by one, then by putting them together into short phrases, and finally by learning to form meaningful sentences.

Playing Sentences

■ In the same way, your musical sentences may not flow easily and naturally in the very beginning. But as you become more comfortable with your playing and increasingly in tune with the background music, you'll hear your melody lines begin to evolve into meaningful musical ideas.

And remember that each and every time you play with *Instant Blues*—for that matter, each and every time you so much as *listen* to the background tape—you're educating your ear and expanding your musical instinct.

So turn on any piece that strikes your fancy and pick a particular set of notes—as few as three will do. Play around with the following suggestions to demonstrate for yourself how varying the *way* you play the same notes can change the entire flavor of your melodies.

Pause!

A good way to gear yourself toward creating musical sentences is simply to take a breather every now and then. Leave some space after every few notes. This will not only give you pause to check in with the background music, but it will keep your notes from rambling on. Avoid the tendency many beginners have to cram several notes together. In fact, if you must err in any direction, play *too few* notes and leave *too much* space.

Accent

You'll need a touch-sensitive instrument to try this out. Emphasize certain notes by playing them *louder* and more forcefully than others; try playing other notes exceptionally *soft*. This will add variety to your music and prevent it from sounding monotonous.

Crescendo and Decrescendo

You can highlight sections of your music by building to a crescendo. Begin playing softly, *gradually increasing the volume*. Decrescendo by doing the opposite: begin playing loudly, then *gradually decrease the volume*.

Loud and Soft

Here's another way you can use volume to add drama to your music. Try playing an *entire section loud*, followed by an *entire section soft*. If we return to our speaker analogy, think about how some ideas are introduced for several paragraphs in a low whisper. Then suddenly the "point" is conveyed in a loud shout. The contrast can be a real attention grabber.

High and Low

Sometimes simply changing the placement of your hands on the keyboard can add interest to your playing. One way to build excitement is to begin by playing a musical phrase on the lower (left) part of the keyboard. When you've completed your thought, move your hands a little higher (to the right) on the keyboard for your next idea, and continue moving up.

Another way to move is in big skips, playing for a while on higher notes, then skipping way back down, or vice versa.

Fast and Slow

You can easily vary the mood of your music by playing several notes as quickly as you're able in some sections and playing slowly and sparsely in others.

Smooth and Choppy

Pick your fingers up quickly off the keys for a brisk, choppy sound; hold them down longer for a smoother, more connected effect. Spice up your playing by alternating between both these techniques.

A Note About the Sustain Pedal

■ The sustain pedal is not used much in blues music, since the echoey, wafting effect it creates is not usually consistent with a blues feel.

Beginners have a tendency to hide behind the pedal, overusing and abusing it in the erroneous belief that it improves the sound of their playing. But more often than not it simply muddies it up. So unless you're experienced at using the pedal, we suggest that you approach it with caution when playing along with *Instant Blues*.

However, if you'd like to play around with the pedal just to see what it does, go for it. It's located at the far right of the pedals at the foot of an acoustic piano. Most electric keyboards have attachable sustain pedals. As the name implies, depressing the pedal will sustain, or stretch out, the sound of the notes being played.

Putting It All Together

■ Keep in mind that no single one of these techniques has any special magic to it. They're simply nuts and bolts that can help hold your musical ideas together. That's why, if you're a complete beginner, experimenting with them is bound to feel mechanical, even awkward, at first.

But if you play around with them for a while, they will quite naturally begin to mesh together, ebbing and flowing spontaneously in the course of your music. You'll find yourself accenting the point of your musical sentences, whispering subtle melodic ideas, and crescendoing to climactic peaks without having to stop and give it so much as a moment's thought.

Chapter 8
Lend Us Your Ear

I n the same way that playing an instrument is a form of expression similar to speaking, playing with other musicians is very
much like carrying on a conversation with a group of friends. A
good musician, like a good conversationalist, is first and foremost
a sensitive listener. He or she remains in tune with the rhythm,
flow, and context of the conversation.

Musical Conversations

■ When professional musicians play together—whether they're
playing a composed orchestral piece or a jazz improvisation—
they're actually having a *musical conversation*. In order for the
interchange to be a free-flowing discourse of musical ideas that
blend well and sound good, each of the musicians must maintain a
continual balance of listening and responding. A band that doesn't
communicate will create music that sounds disjointed and out of
sync and is probably not a band you'd want to listen to for long.

"Conversing" with Your Blues Band

■ It's fine to march to the beat of your own drummer, as long as your drummer is the only musician in the band! But when you're playing along with *Instant Blues* you are, in effect, jamming with your own personal blues band. And in order to fully capture the joy of improvising you'll need to be able to *listen* to the other members in the band.

Experience has shown us that a common pitfall of beginners is that they become so involved in which notes to play, how many to play, and how fast or loud to play them that they simply forget to listen to the music. But with a little practice, listening is a fairly easy skill to acquire.

Learning to Listen

■ While we won't be focusing on formal ear training here, we've outlined a few techniques that can be of use in sharpening your listening skills.

The Art of Just Listening

■ Your brain is capable of absorbing an amazing bank of musical knowledge through nonintellectual, sensory education. That's how, without even trying, you often find yourself singing the lyrics to a song you've heard only a few times or reproducing a particular sax riff in your head long after you've turned off the music.

Start by just listening in a laid back, relaxed, "right brained" sort of way. Simply pop the *Instant Blues* cassette into your tape deck. Choose a piece that suits your mood and listen to it in the same way that you might listen to any one of your favorite recordings. Sit back, relax, and let the music fill your senses. If the spirit moves you, get up and dance, sing along, or even pick up your "baton" and conduct the band!

What Do You Hear?

■ Now listen again, but this time begin to tune in to some of the specifics of the music. You needn't overanalyze them. Simply observe, as if you were taking a leisurely walk down a charming street in a foreign city, enjoying the architecture of the buildings as you stroll along.

Listen for the "architecture" of the music. How is the piece structured? Is there an introduction? Does the piece seem to be divided into sections? How does it end?

What instruments do you hear? Follow the drums for a while,

then the bass. Are there any horns? Do you hear a keyboard part? A guitar? Try to identify and follow all of the instruments you hear.

Listen for Hidden Treasures

■ Throughout the music on the cassette we've buried all sorts of hidden treasures—a rhythmic riff here, a bass line there, and some melodic phrases and musical sentences sprinkled throughout the pieces.

These hidden treasures can provide you with clues to help you become conversant in the language of the blues. Use them in the way that suits you best—to stimulate your own creativity, to set the tone for your own improvisations, or to guide your part of the musical conversations. You can try to copy them exactly, copy the "feel" of them, respond to them, or simply lay back and listen to them.

Using them in any of these ways will go a long way in developing your skill as a musical conversationalist.

Let Your Instinct Be Your Guide

■ Remember, there really are *no hard and fast rules* here. B. B. King wouldn't improvise to a particular piece in exactly the same way that George Benson would. That's what makes every improviser unique and each improvisation a unique experience.

So let your instinct be your guide. Today you may hear a particular piece in one way, and tomorrow you may hear it in another. Your improvisation to the very same piece of music may well take on an entirely different cast each time you play along.

Now you're ready to apply your listening skills to playing along with the tape.

Listen, Then Play

■ First, pick a tune and alternate between listening and playing. Simply listen for a while, then play for a while. Listen again, then play again. Do this for an entire piece or series of pieces. Eventually you'll feel the two begin to merge naturally.

Listen While You Play

■ Now try playing and listening at the same time, shifting your focus back and forth between the background music and the notes you play.

First, focus on the music. Let your fingers move along the keys without giving any special thought to where they land. Think of the notes you play as secondary, almost incidental. Next, shift your focus to the notes you play, making the music incidental.

Go back and forth between concentrating on listening and concentrating on playing. Before long you'll most likely find that you're easily able to listen *while* you play.

One-Way Jam

■ Jamming along with a tape is, of course, only a one-way conversation, since the musicians on the tape can't hear or respond to *you*. But since you're playing with pros, learning how to fit in to their conversation and listening with an ear toward acquiring their "musical accent" is a terrific learning experience in and of itself—a lot like learning French or Spanish from a foreign language tape.

And once you've mastered the invaluable listening skills you're building here, we guarantee that you'll never play *or* listen to music in quite the same way again!

Chapter 9
Building a Blues Story

It's ironic that the blues, which began its evolution on slave plantations, had such a powerfully liberating effect on twentieth century music. By daring to break all the rules, the blues infused music with a new depth of emotion and freedom of expression.

In stark contrast to the perky "Oh Susanna" musical standards of the late nineteenth century, blues lyrics spoke of genuine, complex human emotions. And unlike the clean melodies and clear singing voices of the past, the musical messages of the blues were conveyed in deep, gut-wrenching, throaty growls and framed in driving, syncopated rhythms.

The blues also broke free of the rigid structural confines of traditional western music. Blues musicians took the liberty of "bending" notes to suit their melodic and emotional needs, actually creating new, literally unheard-of combinations of notes along the way.

Eventually these in-between notes became standard blues notes, and specific combinations of blues notes formed themselves quite nicely into blues scales. These elements combine to create the unmistakable sound of the blues as we know it today.

Twelve-Bar Blues

■ Originally blues music was largely unstructured, its guidelines and parameters limited only to the whims of the particular musicians playing it at the moment. But over the years these free improvisations began to form themselves into fairly distinct structures.

While you're likely to hear eight-bar blues, sixteen-bar blues, and twenty-four-bar blues from time to time (and we've included examples of each of these forms on the cassette), by far the most common is the twelve-bar blues. In fact, twelve-bar blues is so widely accepted as the standard that unless another form is specifically indicated, musicians automatically revert to it when they get together to jam.

Since the early 1900s literally thousands of popular tunes have been recorded in the twelve-bar blues format. These include such well-known classics as W. C. Handy's "St. Louis Blues," Glen Miller's "In the Mood," Bill Haley's "Rock Around the Clock," Elvis Presley's "You Ain't Nothin' But a Hound Dog," Chuck Berry's "Johnny B. Goode," James Brown's "I Feel Good," and Michael Jackson's more contemporary hit "Black or White."

So you've already had enough exposure to twelve-bar blues to have a kind of subconscious familiarity with it. This is why you're able to recognize the blues as a musical style distinct from, say, classical or folk music when you hear it.

There's no need to examine every technical nuance of the twelve-bar blues with a scholar's eye. But gaining a general understanding of this straightforward musical form can provide you with a frame of reference that can help guide your playing.

The traditional blues standard "Goin' to Kansas City" illustrates the simple structure of the twelve-bar blues quite well.

"Goin' to Kansas City"

First Chorus

	Bar 1	**2**	**3**	**4**
Part 1	Goin' to Kansas City,	Kansas City here I	come.	

	Bar 5	**6**	**7**	**8**
Part 2	I said, Kansas City,	Kansas City here I	come.	

	Bar 9	**10**	**11**	**12**
Part 3	They've got some crazy little women there	and I'm gonna get me	one.	

	Bar 1	**2**	**3**	**4**
Part 1	Standin' on the corner	Twelfth Street and	Vine.	

	Bar 5	**6**	**7**	**8**
Part 2	Yeah, I'm gonna be standin' on the corner	Twelfth Street and	Vine.	

	Bar 9	**10**	**11**	**12**
Part 3	With my Kansas City Baby and a	bottle of Kansas City	wine.	

We've written out the lyrics to two choruses of the song to demonstrate how they fit into the twelve-bar form. In blues, a chorus might be compared to a paragraph.

In twelve-bar blues, each chorus is made up of three sentences, or parts. These parts usually follow a predictable order, as illustrated below.

Each of these three parts is spread out over four bars, or measures. Four bars plus four bars plus four bars equals twelve bars.

Part one *states* the idea:

Goin' to Kansas City, Kansas City here I come

Part two *repeats and emphasizes* the idea:

I said, Kansas City, Kansas City here I come.

Part three *completes or resolves* the idea:

*They've got some crazy little women there
And I'm gonna get me one.*

Call and Response

■ The *call and response* pattern (the interplay between a lead singer and a group) was derived from African music and is still an integral part of the twelve-bar blues form.

If you take a look at part one of the "Kansas City" diagram, you'll see that the idea, or the *call*, is stated in the first half (bars one and two). Usually the soloist leaves space in the second half (bars three and four) for the *response*, which can be instrumental (such as a horn, guitar, or keyboard riff) or vocal ("I hear you," "Tell it to me!" "Yeah, yeah, yeah").

The call and response pattern is repeated in parts two and three in a similar fashion.

Musical Stories

■ We've used the lyrics to "Kansas City" to illustrate the three-part form. Now let's take a look at how you can use this format *instrumentally*, using notes instead of words to tell a musical story.

"Switchin'," the last piece on Side 2, is a good example of the twelve-bar format. You'll hear "switchin'" sung at the end of each chorus to remind you to alternate from black to white keys or vice versa. This also will help you to get a feel for where the choruses change without having to count out the twelve bars.

The three parts within each chorus can be more difficult to detect at first. That's why we've provided you with some concrete examples. You'll find solos played in the three-part form for the entire second choruses of both "Switchin' " and "Kinda Straight." In both of these pieces we've made the three-part form obvious. You'll hear the musical idea stated in part one, restated in part two, and concluded in part three.

Once you're comfortable with your ability to hear the three parts within the twelve-bar blues format, you're ready to try to tell a musical story of your own!

Part One

Try it first with "Switchin'," since the choruses are so easily identifiable. Begin slowly and easily, playing a short, simple sentence for part one.

Part Two

Play it again! Remember, part two repeats the same idea, sometimes note for note, sometimes with slight alterations, but always with a little more tension or emphasis.

Part Three

When part three comes around, play a few notes to round out the chorus. This doesn't have to be a grand finale. Just try to come to what feels like some kind of completion or conclusion. If you're new at this you can even repeat what you did in parts one and two.

At the end of part three you'll hear "switchin'," reminding you that a new chorus is coming up.

Other twelve-bar pieces that you might enjoy trying this with are "Kinda Straight" and "Ebony Blue" on Side 1 and "Work It Out" on Side 2.

"Lonely Street" on Side 2 is another twelve-bar blues piece, but since it's slower in tempo you might find it a little more difficult to distinguish the different sections at first. However, finding the three parts within "Nice 'n Easy," a slow twelve-bar blues piece on Side 1, really *is* nice and easy, since the singing is done in the three-part form and repeats the same idea three times.

Eight-, Sixteen-, and Twenty-four-Bar Blues

Eight-Bar Blues ("Lazy Bones," Side 1; "Beat So Strong," Side 2)

Unlike twelve-bar blues, eight-bar blues is not divided into three parts. Each chorus is a distinct idea, expressed in one or more sentences. Even if you don't count the bars you'll most likely be able to distinguish between the different choruses.

Sixteen-Bar Blues ("Lady Honeydew," Side 2)

While parts one and two are identical to the twelve-bar blues format, part three is extended by four bars, accounting for the total of sixteen bars.

Twenty-four-Bar Blues ("Let It Ride," Side 2)

This form is similar to twelve-bar blues, except that each of the three parts is twice as long.

The Many Shades of Blue

■ Since the blues is a living, breathing, ever-expanding form, musicians can put their own unique stamps on it. Jazz musicians may use more complex melodies and harmonies in their improvisations. Rock musicians may crank up the volume and vary the beat. Latin musicians may add their own special flavor, using additional percussion and syncopation.

But no matter how it is played, no matter what instruments are used, whether it is played by professional bluesmen at a concert or a group of amateurs jamming in a loft, this vibrant musical style continues to influence virtually every form of American music.

Chapter 10
Singin' the Blues

When I got Instant Blues
I thought what I was gonna do was play

Yeah I said, when I got Instant Blues
All I really wanted *to do was play!*

Now they're tellin' me to sing
I think I'll put this book away!

W ait—stop—don't do it! While *singing* the blues is not in any
way a prerequisite for *playing* the blues, we've included this
chapter as an added bonus that we think you'll enjoy.

Blues lyrics *can* be serious, but they don't have to be; you can
tailor them to fit your mood at the moment. And if rhyming doesn't
come naturally to you, we'll show you how to go about developing
the skill and even how to have to fun singing the blues without
68 rhyming at all!

By the way, you don't have to be a professional singer to sing the blues. In fact, many trained singers actually strive to "un-train" their voices in order to capture the uniquely charismatic guttural, throaty qualities of the blues.

So don't panic. No experience is necessary! You don't need a trained voice, singing lessons, or practice. As a matter of fact, you've already had all the practice you need. You began practicing the call and response pattern in your crib. If you don't believe us, just ask your mother!

All you need is the *Instant Blues* tape, a little gentle guidance, and a story to tell. (And who doesn't have one?)

African-American slaves, the original blues singers, began the development of this form of vocal expression as they labored under the watchful eye of the driver, who encouraged their singing in the belief that it would increase productivity. Since these "work songs" evolved under such oppressive and frustrating circumstances, it's understandable that a pattern of building tension, then releasing it, is a central theme of the blues. And this pattern happens to be one of the things that makes singing the blues such a satisfying experience.

Singing in the twelve-bar blues format gives you a chance not only to state and *restate* your frustration or problem and be cheered on while doing so ("I hear ya talkin'!"), but to actually *resolve* the issue right then and there. There probably aren't many opportunities in life for that kind of instant gratification!

Once you get the hang of it, telling your own personal stories within the three-part structure can be a hypnotic, mesmerizing, and, some believe, even cathartic experience.

Scat It

■ *Scatting* simply means stringing together nonsense syllables. It's not only a great way to get loose, but an art form all its own, as you already know if you've ever heard Ella Fitzgerald, Louis Armstrong, or Sarah Vaughan do it. Even the "shooby do-ing" fifties rock singers did their fair share of scatting.

The jazz feel of "Ebony Blue" makes it an ideal piece to try this out with. In fact, we did a little three-part scatting of our own toward the end. First, listen to the music until you get a feel for the three parts in each chorus. Then scat it.

Don't worry about rhyming or sounding professional. You needn't even confine yourself to the three-part form. As you can hear in "Kansas Boogie," blues scatting can also be unstructured phrases, grunts, groans, or guttural sounds that only hint at an emotion.

The idea here is just to get your mouth open and some sound coming out of it. Just try to jam rhythmically with your voice. Grunt it, groan it, or even scream it, James Brown style.

Talk It

■ Now try putting together some sentences. If you're new at this, you don't even have to sing them. Just talk them at first, without worrying about rhyming or even making sense. Say any old thing that comes to mind. When part two comes around, repeat the same sentence with a little extra *oomph*. For part three, say another sentence or two that you feel completes the thought. Again, anything will do, even:

Part one: *My name is Joe Smith
and I'm tryin' to sing the blues*

Part two: *Yeah, my name is Joe Smith
and I'm tryin' to sing the blues*

Part three: *I may not sound so great yet
but if I keep at it maybe I will*

Rhymes Without Rhyme or Reason

■ There are many ways to say or imply the same idea, which is why rhyming can begin to come naturally with a little practice. You've probably heard blues singers or rap singers go on rhyming *forever* without missing a beat.

If you enjoyed scatting, you can start out by making "scat rhymes." It's simple. Just scat nonsense syllables that rhyme in the three-part form.

Another way to get into the habit of rhyming is to make up silly rhymes, rhymes that have no rhyme or reason. For this exercise, don't worry about completing your idea, just think of a way to rhyme it. For instance:

Part one: *My name is Joe Smith*
and I'm tryin' to sing the blues

Part two: *Yeah, my name is Joe Smith*
and I'm tryin' to sing the blues

Part three: *I'm getting kinda tired*
so I think I'll take a snooze

Rhythm and Rhyme

■ Believe it or not, if you stick with this for any time at all, eventually your blues singing will take on a life of its own. You'll be able to put together complete thoughts and sing them in rhythm—and rhyme!

For instance, you may end up with something like:

My name is Joe Smith
and I'm tryin' to sing the blues

I said my name is Joe Smith
and I can't believe *I'm singin' the blues*

I've got so many rhymes now
I can't decide which one to use

or

When I got Instant Blues
I thought what I was gonna do was play

Yeah, when I got Instant Blues
All I really wanted *to do was play!*

Now I'm glad *I started singin'*
I've got an awful lot to say!

Chapter 11
Look Ma! Two Hands!

As much fun as jamming with one hand can be, most beginners eventually begin to long for the sense of gratification that playing with both hands can bring. Right about now, many of you are probably wishing that we had a second magic wand to wave that would make two-handed playing just as "instant" as we've made one-handed playing.

Well, while we may not be able to transform you into a two-handed virtuoso overnight, we do have some simple bass notes for you to try out that we think are pretty magical! They're easy to manage, sound great with two of the background pieces, and will give you a pleasant little taste of what it feels like to make music with both hands.

Bringing the Left Hand into Play

■ Keyboard players usually use their left hand to play rhythmic bass lines, while playing melodies with the right hand. Here we'll show you the simplest bass line of all, one that uses only a single note!

The Black Keys

■ We'll begin with E♭ as our one-note bass line. Pick an E♭ toward the *lower* half of your keyboard.

E♭

Put on "Just One Thing." We've arranged it so that you can stay on E♭ with the left hand from beginning to end, while playing any black key in the right.

Begin by playing with the left hand only. For now, don't worry about *when* to strike the E♭. Just play it freely, whenever you feel like it. Improvise rhythmically, as if you were a drummer or bass player jamming with a band.

When you're ready, add the *right* hand. Stay on E♭ with the left hand and improvise on any of the black keys in the right. *Keep it very, very simple at first*, playing the left hand only occasionally.

Two Hands and Ten Thumbs?

■ Playing with two hands isn't easy at first. The right hand tends to want to mimic the movement going on in the left hand. Here are a few exercises that can help you develop some coordination.

Tap on Your Lap

Turn on the music and find the beat. Tap to it on your lap with both hands. First try tapping with both hands at the same time. Then try alternating your hands, tapping one beat with the left hand, the next with the right, and so on.

Next, while keeping a steady rhythm with the left hand, tap twice with the right hand for every beat you tap with the left. Finally, while continuing your steady beat with the left hand, begin to improvise rhythms freely with the right hand.

As your skill increases you'll be able to keep a rock-steady beat with the left hand while tapping all sorts of complex rhythms with the right. And this is a skill that transfers beautifully to the keyboard!

Drum It

Now go to the keyboard. Put a finger of the left hand on a low E♭ and a finger of the right hand on one of the higher E♭'s.

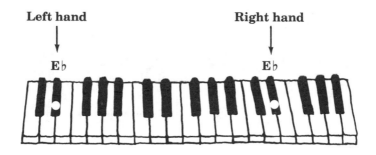

Left hand   Right hand

E♭   E♭

Begin by drumming rhythmically on the keys in the same way as you just tapped on your lap. Make up your own rhythmic combinations as you play.

Once you get comfortable with this, try adding any second black key with the right hand, so that you'll be drumming on E♭ with the left hand and *two* black keys with the right. Work your way up to as many black keys with the right hand as you can handle comfortably, while staying on E♭ with the left. After a while you'll be able to let your right hand go and play freely on any of the black keys, even adding the white key A if you wish.

The White Keys

■ Now try it on the white keys. We've arranged "Tunnel Vision" on Side 2 of the tape so that throughout the piece, D works as the one-note bass line with the left hand along with any white key with the right hand.

Put on "Tunnel Vision" and play along. Begin slow and easy, just as you did with the black keys. Play the D with the left hand alone for a while, then add the right and let loose!

The Long and Short of Two-Handed Playing

■ If you have some experience at the keyboard, look in appendix B. There you'll find chord progressions and bass notes for each of the pieces on the tape.

If you're a beginner who'd like to be able to manage these chord progressions, don't hesitate to seek some assistance from a teacher or a more advanced friend.

You see, there's a long and short of two-handed playing. The long of it is that making flowing music with both hands just doesn't come overnight. The mastery of any skill requires a fairly long road of practice, patience, and persistence.

But the short of it is that if you spend even a short time playing around with the coordination exercises and the simple bass lines we've given you, and you continue to play around with *Instant Blues* whenever you feel the need for inspirational guidance along the way, you'll have shortened that road by a long shot!

Chapter 12
How to Play Along on Any Instrument

If you're fortunate enough to have your own personal orchestra in the form of an electronic keyboard or synthesizer, you've probably already discovered just how great other instruments can sound along with the various backgrounds on the cassette. But you don't have to be a keyboard player or even *own* a keyboard to play along.

In fact, *Instant Blues* adapts beautifully to *any instrument!*

We'll tell you which notes will work for your instrument along with Side 1 of the tape and which to use along with Side 2. The notes we'll be giving you can be played in all the registers your instrument can reach. If you don't know the names of the notes on your instrument of choice, you can use a fingering chart or a teacher to help you locate them.

Once you've got the notes, it's easy. Just read the book, follow the instructions as they apply to your instrument, and play the blues!

To play along with "Switchin' " on any of the following instruments, simply alternate between the set of notes designated for Side 1 when playing along with the black key section and the notes designated for Side 2 when playing along with the white key section.

If you have an instrument that can play *chords,* such as guitar, banjo, accordion, or autoharp, look in appendix B, where we have written out the chord progressions you can use to play along with each piece on the tape.

If you play an instrument that's in concert pitch, such as bass, guitar, flute, trombone, bassoon, oboe, or any string instrument, the notes you can use to play along with Side 1 of the tape are:

E♭   G♭   A♭   A   B♭   D♭

For Side 2 of the tape, play along on these notes:

D   F   G   A♭   A   C

If you play a B♭ instrument, such as tenor sax, clarinet, or trumpet, the blues notes for Side 1 are:

F   A♭   B♭   B   C   E♭

For Side 2 of the tape, use:

E   G   A   B♭   B   D

If you play an E♭ instrument, such as alto sax, the blues notes for Side 1 are:

C   E♭   F   G♭   G   B♭

For Side 2 of the tape, use:

B   D   E   F   F♯   A

For more esoteric instruments, contact your teacher!

Chapter 13
Party Games

Instant Blues is guaranteed to make you the life of the party! Once you've dazzled your family and amazed your friends with your mesmerizing melodies, the party games we suggest to you here can make everyone else the life of the party too.

These games also happen to be great family activities. Use them to inspire and motivate your kids by introducing them to the fun and exciting adventure of making music!

Making Beautiful Music Together

■   There are lots of ways two or more people of any age or level of experience can make beautiful music together.

Two-Way Jam

When you play along with the *Instant Blues* cassette by yourself, you're having, in a sense, a one-way jam, communicating with a group of musicians whom you can hear but who can't hear you. Here's your chance to have a two-way jam along with a real live person who can actually hear and respond to the notes you play!

Here's how. Pick a partner and a background piece and simply take turns playing melodies back and forth. Try to really "talk to each other." Explore and experiment with all sorts of musical ideas! Who knows? Your collaboration may just result in a Grammy Award–winning piece of music. Well, okay, maybe not. But at the very least, with a little patience and persistence, you'll likely find yourself immersed in a sparkling musical conversation.

And by the way, if you can wangle an accomplished musician into your musical buddy system, this could be one two-way jam that just might prove downright inspirational!

Trading Solos

You've probably attended blues, jazz, or rock concerts where you've watched all of the band members take turns playing solos. If you have friends who play instruments other than keyboards, you can do this too. Show your friends chapter 12, which explains exactly how to use *Instant Blues* with other instruments, then turn on the tape and jam!

You can take turns playing solos with your friends even if you have only one keyboard. Play a melody along with the music for a while, then step aside and let the next person play. The solos can be of a prearranged length or as long or as short as each person chooses.

If you're using a synthesizer you might pick a new sound for each new solo.

Copy Cat

This game is a great ear-training, memory, and concentration exercise. Play a simple melody on keyboard or on any other instrument. Then let someone try to copy it. You can keep it simple. Or for a really challenging competition, take turns increasing the level of complexity as you go along.

Guess Who?

This game can be a lot of laughs and is guaranteed to give those stuffy, stern internal judges of yours a good kick in the pants. Take turns performing for each other, adopting the persona and stage presence of a well-known celebrity, musical or otherwise, or a mutual acquaintance, well loved or otherwise. Then, guess what? Guess who!

Bass Lines for Buddies

While one beginner may have it tough coordinating bass lines in the left hand and melodies in the right, two beginners have it a heck of a lot easier! Put on "Just One Thing" on Side 1 or "Tunnel Vision" on Side 2. Let one person improvise rhythmically on the simple one-note bass lines—E♭ for "Just One Thing" and D for "Tunnel Vision"—while another plays the melodies. After a while, switch sides.

Any experienced musicians in the house? If so, they can play the more complex bass lines found in appendix B while the less experienced players make the melodies.

Twelve-Bar Blues Games

Using our "Singin' the Blues" chapter as your guide and "Switchin'," "Kansas Boogie," or any of the twelve-bar blues pieces as backgrounds, take turns singing or talking in the three-part form, making up rhymes about other people in the room, people you know in common, political figures, or anyone or anything else that comes to mind. Something like:

Part one: *There's a lady in the corner*
all dressed in red

Part two: *I see a lady in the corner*
she's all dressed in red

Part three: *I'd like to tell her she looks pretty*
but it might go to her head

For a variation on the theme, begin with one person singing the first two parts and another finishing the thought, creating the third part, quite literally, on the spot.

Both of these games can be just as much fun, and sometimes even funnier, if you get stuck. Then just finish the thought any old way, either with a nonsense rhyme or without rhyming at all. Sometimes the sillier and the more out of context part three becomes, the better.

Hit the Road, Jack

You can pack up your family, friends, and, thanks to transistor batteries, your cassette player, your keyboard, and the *Instant Blues* tape, and take them to the beach or the park for an afternoon of musical fun and games.

Go Play in the Street!

If you're *really* feeling adventurous, here's a game you can play all on your own. Set yourself up on a street corner, flip on the tape, wow passersby with your mellifluous melodies, and wait to be discovered, either by the head of a major record label or a local law enforcement official!

Chapter 14
A Final Note

Now that you've read through the book and played through the tape, it's time to stop and reflect on what the experience has meant for you and where you might want to go from here. Perhaps we can help.

We have some good news, some even better news, and some not-so-bad news.

You've probably already discovered most of the good news. You now know firsthand what it takes most musicians years of pondering music theory and practicing scales to find out—just how good it feels to really swing, to make real blues music without having to stop and think about a single thing!

And because each encounter with every piece is a brand new, spontaneous experience, *Instant Blues* can always serve as a creative companion to provide you with a stimulating source of musical gratification or as an upbeat musical toy to share with others for fun and games. In other words, you can get the blues any ole' time you want!

The even better news is that as a result of simply jamming along with the tape, you now know more about the meaning, the structure, and the feel of the blues than you've yet to even realize. And because of the insights you've gained, your musical senses will forever be more alert, your ears more attuned, your sense of rhythm more acute.

And not only that, but you've garnered all of this instinctual knowledge without even having to work much at it. Come to think of it, you've made quite an astute investment in your musical future—you've gotten quite a bit of something for just about nothing.

Now for the not-so-bad news. Say you've become so turned on to making music that *Instant Blues* just isn't enough for you. Perhaps you want to go on and become a master blues musician, or maybe you'd like to add classical, jazz, or country to your repertoire. Well, as with the mastery of any skill, it'll take study, practice, and dedication.

But, believe it or not, practicing can be fun! With the right elements brought into balance, you really *can* be free to enjoy the scenery along the exciting and stimulating journey that studying music can be. What you'll need is a patient and joyous approach, a positive, enthusiastic attitude, and a competent and supportive teacher to guide you. If you're enjoying the lessons, it's generally safe to assume that you've found the right teacher and the right approach.

And when you *do* find the right teacher, be sure to bring *Instant Blues* along. In appendix C we've included tips for teachers, especially designed to help them help you.

Now that's not so bad, is it?

Appendix A
The ABC's of Music

I f your left brain is screaming out for knowledge, knowledge, knowledge, then this bonus section is for you. Here we'll show you a few keyboard basics and give you chord progressions that you can use along with the backgrounds, if and when you're ready for them. If you're a teacher, here's where you'll find some tips on how to use *Instant Blues* to enhance the learning process for your students.

You don't have to know the names of the notes on the keyboard to use this book, but if you *want* to know them, they're really quite simple to learn. In fact, it's as easy as A B C D E F G—the only letters used in music.

Let's begin by taking a close look at the black keys. By now you've probably noticed that they're divided into groups of twos and threes all the way across the keyboard.

Locate a group of any three black keys. The white key between

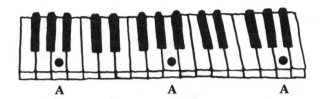

the second and third of the black keys is always called A, wherever it appears on the keyboard.

A B C D E F G A B etc.

As you can see, from here on, things become very logical.

Up and Down

■ As the notes move to the *right*, they get *higher*. This is referred to as moving "up" on the keyboard. As they move to the *left*, they get *lower*, and this is referred to as moving "down" on the keyboard.

Just remember: *r*ight *r*aises, *l*eft *l*owers.

Octaves

■ Every note repeats itself *eight* notes away. The distance between them is called an *octave*. From one A to the next one is an octave, from B to B is an octave, from C to C is an octave, and so on.

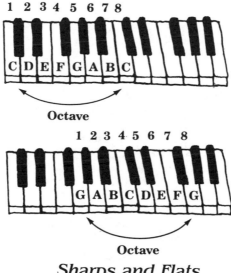

Sharps and Flats

■ Notes can be referred to as sharps or flats. A flat symbol (♭) next to a note means you should play the note directly to the *left* of it, whether it's black or white.

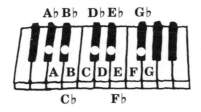

A sharp symbol (♯) next to a note means you should play the note directly to the *right* of it, whether it's black or white.

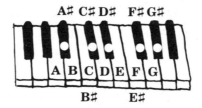

As you can see, every black note, and even some of the white notes, can be called by either sharp or flat names. In fact, on the piano, the same key can have both a sharp and a flat name. If you look at the diagrams of the sharps and the flats, you will see that E♭ can also be called D♯.

Appendix B
Chords

A *chord* is generally defined as a group of three or more notes played together. For those of you with some experience, we've included the lead sheets (chord progressions) for all of the pieces on the cassette.

We've simplified them so that most of the chords are either major or minor and have included diagrams of all of the chords that appear in the lead sheets.

If you're a beginner, all of this may seem overwhelming. But with a little help from a good teacher or an experienced friend, and some practice, it won't be long before you'll be able to have fun playing chords along with the tape.

Chord Diagrams

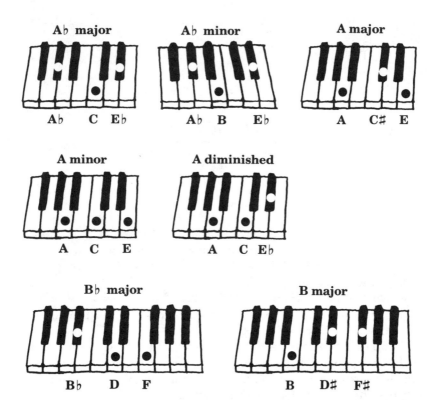

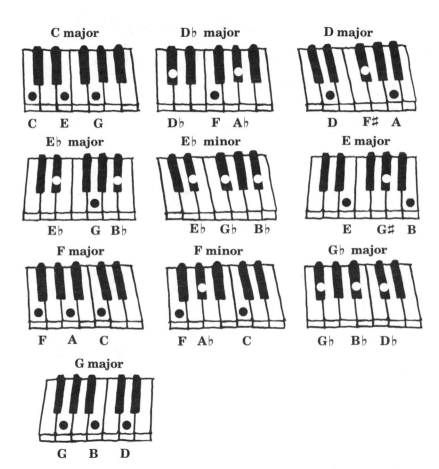

97

Chord Progressions—Side 1

<u>Kansas Boogie</u> (Side 1, piece 1)

Introduction

Lazy Bones (Side 1, piece 2)

Introduction

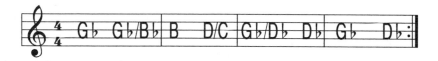

Nice 'n Easy (Side 1, piece 3)

Introduction

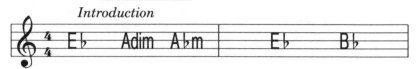

Kinda Straight (Side 1, piece 4)

A Minor Affair (Side 1, piece 5)

Introduction

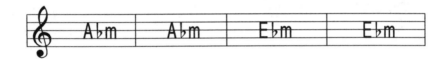

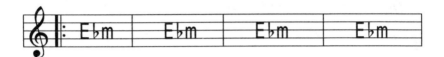

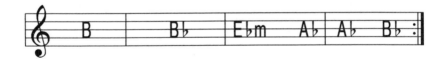

Ebony Blue (Side 1, piece 6)

Just One Thing (Side 1, piece 7)

Repeat E♭ minor chord for the entire piece

| 4/4 E♭m | E♭m | E♭m | E♭m |

Chord Progressions—Side 2

Beat So Strong (Side 2, piece 1)

| 4/4 D | D | G | G |

| D | A | D | D |

Let It Ride (Side 2, piece 2)

Lonely Street (Side 2, piece 3)

Work It Out (Side 2, piece 4)

107

Lady Honeydew (Side 2, piece 5)

Introduction

Tunnel Vision (Side 2, piece 6)

Repeat D major chord for the entire piece

Switchin' (Side 2, piece 7)

White keys

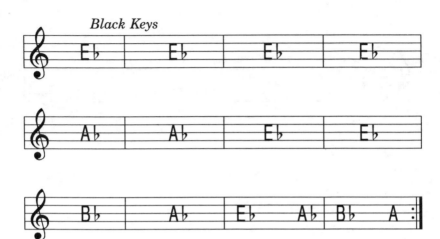

Black Keys

110

Appendix C
Tips for Teachers

The *Instant Blues* system can provide a powerful motivational tool for students when used in conjunction with traditional teaching techniques. While this book does not purport to be the meat and potatoes of music making, it can be used as an irresistible hors d'oeuvre at the outset of a lesson or practice session to whet your student's appetite or as a tantalizing dessert at the end.

As most teachers have experienced, exposing beginners exclusively to traditional teaching methods can serve as a major stumbling block. Many music books designed for beginners contain unfamiliar songs that are either too difficult to play or too simple to sound good. So the once enthusiastic student all too often becomes discouraged and demoralized.

While a serious music student won't be daunted by any of this and will diligently persist in perfecting every aspect of study necessary to becoming a professional musician, there exists quite a substantial bank of potential music makers out there whose needs are sadly going unmet.

These are most often adult or teenaged beginners who genuinely love music and want to participate in making it. But frustration sets in quickly as they begin to realize that they may have months or years of scales, drills, and unappealing method books ahead of them.

For many, this frustration could be offset so easily, simply by supplementing the necessary but tedious tasks with the kind of excitement and immediate gratification that *Instant Blues* provides. Unpressured, free improvisation is often just the key to keeping students inspired and motivated along the way.

Some students may even discover that improvisation is enough to satisfy their need for a musical outlet. And in those cases *Instant Blues* actually *can* provide the main course, as there are so many creative and exciting ways to work—and *play*—with it.

We'll suggest ways in which you can use the *Instant Blues* book and cassette package to reach students of many different levels and needs.

First, a word about why *Instant Blues* works.

Side 1

■ Quite simply, with the exception of "Lazy Bones," all of the pieces on Side 1 are recorded in either the E♭ dorian or E♭ mixolydian modes. The five black notes, E♭, G♭, A♭, B♭, and D♭, along with the one white note, A, make up the *E♭ blues scale*, which can work equally well with both of these modes.

"Lazy Bones" is recorded in the key of G♭ major. Here the five black notes make up the *G♭ pentatonic scale*, while the A natural is the flatted third of the scale, one of the most common blues notes.

Side 2

■ All of the pieces on Side 2, with the exception of "Switchin'," are recorded in D mixolydian. Since the D blues scale consists of D, F, G, A♭, A, and C, these notes will all sound right when played along with Side 2. Although the two white notes E and B won't sound as bluesy, they will not clash with any of the backgrounds and can, in fact, sound quite interesting, since both are a part of the D mixolydian mode.

"Switchin' " simply switches between D and E♭ mixolydian.

Music Theory

■ *Instant Blues* can be a useful tool for exploring various elements of music theory with your students. It can be used to demonstrate how to count beats, play in rhythm, play chords, and arrange music from lead sheets, as well as the basic elements of the blues—including blues notes and scales and the various blues progressions.

We've simplified the chords on the lead sheets to basic triads in order to make them less intimidating for the beginner. More advanced students can be shown how to add sevenths, ninths, and thirteenths for a fuller, richer sound.

Coordination

■ You can help students improve their coordination, using either the chords contained in the lead sheets or even just the root of each chord.

By teaching students to improvise with the right hand over left-hand bass lines of increasing complexity (first whole notes, then half notes, then quarter notes, and eventually even syncopated bass lines), you can help them develop independence of the hands in a way that they'll enjoy far more than traditional drills.

Ear Training

■ Your students can greatly improve their ears by learning to play along with the chord changes. More advanced students can attempt to hear and copy the bass lines or some of the melodies used on the *Instant Blues* cassette.

Comping

■ To help your students enjoy playing along with the tape and to introduce them to accompaniment, have them play the root of each chord with the left hand and the full chord with the right hand, as if accompanying a band. Help them to add and vary rhythms as they become more proficient.

Songwriting and Composing

■ Those students who are interested can be given assignments to create bass lines of their own and compose melodies, lyrics, and even complete songs to the various backgrounds. In this exercise students can be encouraged to experiment with notes other than the "foolproof" ones we've identified in the book.

Jam with Your Students

■ One of the most powerful ways of using *Instant Blues* with your students is simply to jam with them. Trade two bars, four bars, and even entire choruses. Your influence and input will go a long way in developing their feel for the blues and for music in general, as well as in assisting them to recognize and create cohesive melodies within the framework of their own ability.